SILVIVAL:

CONFESSIONS OF A SILVER SNIPER

VICTOR DALCENORI

2012

SILVIVAL: CONFESSIONS OF A SILVER SNIPER

SILVIVAL: CONFESSIONS OF A SILVER SNIPER

Economic doom and gloom throughout the world has people searching for order to the chaos. There is not one definitive order which all agree on, but, many have defined precious metals, and more specifically, silver, as a potential savior.

This book is about Silvival. Silvival means: utilizing silver as a means to ensure your economic survival and, ultimately, your overall survival. The hero of this story doesn't take on minions of evil. Rather, the hero is an individual like you or me, who simply goes about searching for ways to ensure survival today, tomorrow, and forever. Silver just so happens to be the method of survival utilized, thus the reason for the development of the word, silvival. It means so much that a word had to be designed to describe it! Plus, it was a lot easier than saying "silver survival" or "silver for survival" or "silver as a means for economic and overall survival" all the time! I think you get the point. You'll definitely want to explore the means taken to ensure SILVIVAL!

This book will enable all readers to find their own path to silvival. Through the various techniques mentioned, combined with an easy tracker for personal analysis, the reader will be able to obtain the skills necessary to become a silver sniper. Silver sniping will become a vital skill needed to find, purchase, and maintain silver inventory in any market. That and many other silvival techniques will be learned and mastered through the use of this book.

Chapter 1: The Silver Lining

Just like most other days, we exchanged emails with the purpose of sharing our ideas on things going on in our lives. On these days, though, there was a deeper meaning behind the sharing of ideas. The following are excerpts from those emails. Well worth sharing with more than just us. Enjoy!

Silvival means: utilizing silver as a means to ensure your economic survival and, ultimately, your overall survival.

I know you're probably growing sick of me mentioning it, dude, but, here's where I'm coming from with this...

I've wanted to be a businessman who earned millions by investing in stocks and real estate since I was a teen. My fave movie was Wall Street (1987). I read everything by Donald Trump when I graduated high school. I wanted to follow in that path. I wanted to be rich. It's been a motivating force in my life for 25 years. ONE PROBLEM: I WAS NEVER IN A PROPER POSITION TO TAKE ADVANTAGE OF OPPORTUNITIES! Like Microsoft came out in 1985. I wanted to invest in 1987 but didn't have the means. I don't even want to say what I missed out on there. :-(

Numerous opportunities were presented to me! But, the most glaring missed opportunities come in the form of three examples:

1) Priceline: In 2000 I remember telling my manager at Domino's to invest in this IPO (Initial Public Offering) of this new company called Priceline. It wasn't a flippant, "hey, check this out, dude." It was an understanding of the business model and the potential for the company based on research I had been doing at the time. Of course, I didn't have the money to purchase the 100 shares at that time. Had I purchased 100 shares in 2000 at $34.50 per share the stock had a 6:1 split in 2003, which would have increased my original shares to 600 and the value of my investment today would total $354, 246!!!

2) Amazon: As with Priceline, I researched and understood the business model for Amazon. It was in 1999 that I wanted to get in on this company. Had I invested at that time it would have taken me $5500 to purchase 100 shares in January of 1999. The stock split three times that year turning those original 100 shares into 600 shares. Today the value of my purchase would be $107,478!!!

3) Real Estate: The opportunities were presented in 2005 right before my child was born. My business partner and I were in the midst of investing in five properties. The first property we went to the courthouse to see if our valuation of the property we researched was a viable investment. That property sold for $47,000 at the auction. The property value was $125,000. We were going to put $15,000 in to the fix up and re-sell. Had we been able to purchase it for even $50,000 we would have made $50,000 when we sold it as the property sold for $115,000 a year later. After that missed opportunity we negotiated a deal for four rental properties with five rental units. I used a three-prong negotiation technique I developed which funnels the seller to the most profitable agreement for us. Each solution would be profitable but the one we saw as most profitable was the one chosen by the seller. It worked tremendously. Each property was bought under appraised value. It was a real estate investor's dream come true. We would be able to rent out each unit for immediate cash flow and if we wanted to flip these properties our gains would be tremendous, also. My business partner fumbled the ball with our hard money lender and the deals never finalized. Ultimately it was another missed opportunity presented by not being in a position to take advantage of that opportunity. Potential value: $50,000 + $36,000/yr. or if sold all properties the net value would have been at least $500,000!!!

TOTAL VALUE OF THREE MAIN MISSED OPPORTUNITIES: $961,724!!!

Of course, missing out on those three main missed opportunities has had a lasting effect on my psyche. They drive me forward to achieve what I want to achieve financially. Those opportunities could have had a domino effect in creating more successes in my life. Hell, they most definitely would have!!!

Now enter SILVER! I am finally in a position to take advantage of an opportunity presented to me and I'll be damned if I'm going to let it go!!! And I'm telling everyone about it!!! Why? Because it seems to open doors the more you let people know. Like a compounding effect, the thoughts are thrown out there and the laws of attraction take hold. For instance (and this is no lie!!!!), as I was writing this email to you, an associate called me. He knows I'm big into silver as an investment and was talking to his dad about it (his dad is very well-off, too). His dad told him he had just taken a bunch of silver to some guy who put an ad in the paper for purchasing people's silver. This associate then got an idea for me. You see, his dad lives in a retirement community. There are a lot of people like him there that have money but don't want to deal with their "worthless" coins. This associate got the idea for me to pitch to the retirement community to purchase these "worthless" coins. BOOM!!!!

As soon as I'm done here I'm designing a flyer his dad is going to pass around the community for me and I'm going to set up a date and time to go there for the purpose of purchasing their unwanted coins.

I REFUSE TO ALLOW ANOTHER OPPORTUNITY PASS ME BY!!!!

Thus the reason for....SILVIVAL!!!!

I didn't think about investing in this one when it came out but here it is...
Had you invested in 100 shares of Apple in 1984 when it first came out, your initial cash outlay would have been $287. That $287 today would be worth at least......
$428, 328 (that's without reinvesting dividends)
1,492 times your initial investment!!!
WOW!!!!

Hello!

Well, now that you put it that way, I agree with you. I guess when I was thinking about what "investing" meant, I was thinking like $200 or $300. My conundrum, at least one I have created in my mind, is that I owe about $2000 on a credit card, which I have been keeping up with, but I don't like having that accruing interest hanging over my head. So, in my mind, I have made an assumption that if I pick any other way to spend my money, I will lose more money because the interest on the credit card will grow more than what any other investment can provide in growth. Now, that is an uneducated assumption. You know, I don't really know if that's correct.

So, I have been forging ahead at knocking the credit card down to zero, and then wanted to go on to invest....(my $200 and up assumptive definition).

Since you put it that way about buying it in very small denominations, well, now I see I can do both. One thing about me is that because I have so very little knowledge about investing, I have a ton of blind spots or assumptions that I really can't see, sort of like blind spots that I don't understand are there.

As far as being scared of silver...if there is one thing and only one thing to invest in that I fear the least, it's silver :D, and that's based on what you've said, the video link you sent me which was incredible, and the article I read just out of high school. If your house burns down with the silver inside it, the one thing left is your silver. One cannot say that about many other investments, I think, other than precious metals. And you can bury it and find it 40 years later. Hell, if we really had to, we could pound silver into very artistic belt buckles. There is a demand for silver belt buckles out west.

When you get in tonight, I'll either call or email and ask for links on where to buy silver, I mean the places and people you trust. Between silver investments and my writing, I shall have a farm.

I really don't want to let the silver opportunity slip past me.

On Mar 3, 2012, at 8:23 AM, Vic wrote:

Good talk last night, bud. I was a little disturbed, though, by your comment: "When I get a chance I'll invest in silver. I really don't have the money right now." Not to be an asshole, Sir, but that was an uneducated statement. I'm not trying to sell you anything. I'm trying to get you in on a potentially life-changing financial decision. Apparently you don't realize that you can buy silver in MANY denominations. I've bought as little as .032 ounces of silver which is 1 gram. And I bought it for 99 cents!!! The value of that amount of silver is minimal at today's spot price and is equivalent to $1.12. But, the point is, you can invest in silver for almost as little as you are comfortable with. Set aside a dollar per day and by the end of the month you'll have enough to purchase a full ounce or various smaller denominations.

If you're scared to invest in silver. That's ok. Just remember one thing: silver is unlike investing in Microsoft or Apple, in that you can actually invest in silver knowing the intrinsic value will never drop to zero. It can't! And if you buy a coin that has a $10 value on it then, guess what, it can never drop below $10. Paper stocks can bottom out to zero.

I went on that long diatribe to basically say this: "yes, you can buy silver." Open your mind, Bud! If you don't want to buy silver that's one thing. But, if you do, then there are alternative means. If nothing else, you'll have a bright, shiny coin or bar to look at. I know how you go for those shiny things. Lol.

Talk to you later,

Vic
Sent via BlackBerry by AT&T

No problem at all, dude. That's what friends are for. You've given me a wealth of your personal knowledge over the years so I'm glad to repay the favor in any way I can.

It's a good feeling, huh?! There will be plenty more where that came from. Soon you'll be sharing your own personal silvival techniques with me and others. Pay it forward!!! Yeah, starting with the Eagles is the best route to go. Great steal today, dude!!!

Sinsilverly (lmao),

Vic
Sent via BlackBerry by AT&T

-----Original Message-----
From:
Date: Sun, 4 Mar 2012 22:01:07
To:
Subject: Thanks a million!

Hey dude,

Thanks a million for all the advice tonight. It is wonderful to have someone share all his hard work, knowledge and time like that for my betterment. Tonight was just the beginning for me. Yes, I have a lot to learn, but I'll get there. Silvival.

You did all the work and shared it with me out of just friendship. I hope I get have the opportunity to do the same for you.

I made my first ebay grab of silver, and I'll keep my eye open for more as it pops up and stays in my price range. I'll probably stay with the silver eagles for a while, and then once my courage increases, I'll wade into the deeper waters of other silver items.

Thank you very much again for all your help.

Sinsilverly,

Bud Shilver

Hey, Bud! Just wanted to share some more insight on things regarding silver. Here are two articles which reveal that silver, as a market, is being manipulated and why. Not to bring gloom and doom to the investment aspect of silver but to shed light on the future potential of the value (which should be showing the value of it now) of silver. One article is from 2010 and the other is from 2004. Read the 2010 article first then the 2004 article. You get a good look into things which depict a manipulation of prices by those with the power to do so. But, after reading all that, the key point is made in the last sentence of the 2004 article. Therein lies the intrinsic truth to this entire thing and why so many people (me included) are "all in" on this market. Happy reading.
Vic

This is an article from a respected precious metals site, Kitco.com. This is the site I monitor daily and the one I use to give me my spot price for silver. They offer many insights and articles for the entire precious metals market and here is an article which shows you the state of affairs in our country/world in regards to the economy, etc.
Check it out:
http://www.kitco.com/ind/McWhinnie/20120305.html
V

-----Original Message-----
From
Date: Tue, 6 Mar 2012 20:13:26
To:
Subject: Re: Two Important Articles>>>

That was a good one too. At some point, things will have to catch up. It would be nice to be sitting in the catbird seat when that spike hits.

After reading these, I really don't see how a monstrous financial collapse is avoidable. And when it happens, it's all the more reason to have our survival skills well-honed. The world will go bonkers. It's best to ride out that period away from the masses.

I have found some more good stuff for the B.O.B. One is the Silky Pocket Boy folding tree saw. It's from Japan and cuts on the pull and kicks just about anything else's ass. A folding saw, a good knife, and maybe even a tiny knife for intricate carving work making fish hooks, etc., would be an excellent start for our wood processing tools. I'm also thinking about a Snow & Nealley Hudson Bay Axe. I had one but gave it away as a goodbye present to someone else. The head is 1.75lb. That was a good one.

I did some more hand drill work tonight. I am having no luck whatsoever at generating smoke. I'm beginning to suspect my fireboard of not being the right hardness of wood. Maybe it's too hard. I get nothing but a little smoke smell. I want to try a softer fireboard. Maybe that'll help. Dammit my hands are sore. I will not be deterred in this skill. If I can master this one, then it's all the more reason to stay away for the bow drill. That thing has always killed my hip.

I just watched a good video on how to navigate with a broken cell phone. Great stuff!

Bud

On Mar 6, 2012, at 9:12 PM, Vic Dalcenori wrote:

http://www.survivalblog.com/2011/04/using_your_smart_phone_as_a_su.html

Gotta follow this.

This is an article from today off one of the sites I view religiously....http://www.kitco.com/ind/Hunter/20120321.html Two main things I'm looking at in full focus are: 1) All the doomsday prophecy stuff out there pertaining to this year, especially December 21, 2012; and 2) It is an election year. Something is about to go down! Think back to Y2K for a minute. Nothing really happened immediately when the clocks changed to the new year except for some minor computer glitches, but, within 21 months, we had a major attack on our soil in the form of 9/11. Inside job or not, it was a major event which worked to change many things immediately and since. 10 years hence we are facing one thing after another after another. Here, there, and everywhere! Mostly economical. The battle is for control. We have all become controlled by money. Whether we like it or not, money has made us slaves. All of us! We can't do anything without it.

With the signing of the Executive Order mentioned in the article referenced in the link above, my Spidey-sense is telling me we need to be prepared for something major to happen again. This time we all are going to feel it! Nobody will be unaffected. Martial Law is about to be declared, I think. Simply stated: we need to be prepared! How? I'm not exactly sure, but I do believe we need to get back to our days of exploring and trying to get in tune with nature. We need to work diligently on our "survival" skills. Those skills most suited for living a minimalist lifestyle. I don't trust anyone else to aid me in planning for this. Let's try to get together and begin planning for what we will do when the SHTF! We've talked back and forth about doing this and doing that but I'm talking about formulating an EXACT plan.

One where we say: hey, if/when the SHTF this will be our plan of action. Designate a Rally Point. How we're going to get to that Rally Point. What we need to have once we reach that Rally Point, etc., etc. I think we both could formulate something which would not only aid us but could include aiding those near and dear to us. I will tap into my Army days and we can sit down and come up with a plan which basically states what the Tasks, Conditions, and Standards will be in accordance with our ultimate objective which will be: SURVIVAL. I want to tap into your innate understanding of nature combined with your desire to make do with what you're given. I think together we could come up with an ironclad plan of action which could work to help us adapt and overcome the upcoming catastrophes. What say you? Are you in? I'm serious, dude. Preparation is the key and I think we can be the locksmiths! Let me know what you think. Thanks bud.
Vic

Hey, Bud! I went on a spending spree yesterday. I sat in on a webinar about wealth creation and got many confirmations of what I had suspected. Dude!!! You gotta watch out with your money. In these turbulent economic times one thing is for sure...CASH IS TRASH!!! I'm buying silver. Gold is too expensive for my blood right now trading at $1,700+ per ounce. I wish I would have bought some when I first looked at the potential upswing two and a half years ago when it was trading around $700 per ounce. But, I've let too many opportunities pass me by and finally am in a position to do something.

All indicators are pointing to silver outperforming gold anyway. So, with silver trading at $33.28 per ounce I bought me some!!! Now, you're not gonna get it at that spot price anywhere so you have to invest smart. I bought a few items at an average of $40.68 per ounce. You can scour Ebay for items (as I did all night long!) And bid to where you're comfortable. Conservative estimates are saying silver will climb to about $70 per ounce by year-end. Many of the "people in the know" are saying even higher. There are all types of indicators and if you're really interested (which you should be!) I'd be more than willing to show you my research based on these knowledgeable individuals. Anyway, they are predicting silver to GO THROUGH THE ROOF!!!

I'm buying, dude, because all the wealthy people I know (my landlord and his accountant to name two) agree with me that our paper money is going to be worth nothing! Gold and silver is where they're putting their money and silver is looking more appealing as a short and long-term investment. Now's the time! Buy Silver Eagles! I bought six yesterday. They are 1 oz. of pure silver. Anything pure silver is the way to go. I also bought a 10 oz. bar of silver for a great price! If silver gets over just $40 per oz. which should happen shortly, I'll have already recouped my investment. Everything else will be profit on profit on profit!!! Scour Ebay for bargains, dude! Silver coins are good, too. I'm researching and buying.

I'm telling you this because you are my Bud! My best friend! And I don't want you to miss out on this. I would feel sick if I didn't tell you and then you missed out on potential profits, also. Don't fall for the fancy-schmancy $70 charges for special commemorative silver dollar coins, etc. 1 oz. of silver is 1 oz. of silver! It doesn't matter if the coin is a 1993 or a 2012. Yes, some have special value but mostly you're looking at them for silver investment purposes. If you have any questions feel free to ask. I'd love for you to say you profited, also.

Your faithful friend,

Victor
Sent via BlackBerry by AT&T

Chapter 2: Silvival Essential: The Silver Tracker

THE REASON FOR THE TRACKER IS: TO TRACK YOUR PURCHASES, MAINTAIN AN INVENTORY, MONITOR YOUR VALUE OF INVESTMENT, TRACK YOUR PURCHASE PRICE PER OUNCE VS. SPOT PRICE, AND MOST IMPORTANTLY….AID IN ABILITY TO PURCHASE BARGAINS AND QUICKLY ASSESS WHAT TO PURCHASE ITEMS AT TO LOWER YOUR PRICE PER OUNCE>>>>>WORKS TO INCREASE YOUR SPEED IN FIGURING OUT WHAT TO PURCHASE ITEMS FOR ESPECIALLY WITH BIDS ENDING SOON!!! BECOME THE ULTIMATE SILVER SNIPER!!!

THE ULTIMATE SILVER TRACKER IS A SPREADSHEET TO ENABLE YOU TO QUICKLY TARGET PURCHASES AT THE RIGHT PRICE AND ENABLE YOU TO TRACK THOSE PURCHASES AND MAINTAIN AN ACTIVE INVENTORY. I USE THIS VERY TRACKER TO HELP ME KEEP TRACK OF ALL MY PURCHASES AND HAVE HANDY AN INVENTORY OF EVERY ITEM I'VE BOUGHT ON EBAY AND OTHERWISE. FOR THOSE ACTIVELY USING EBAY AS A MEANS TO PURCHASE SILVER AT DISCOUNTED PRICES, THE "SILVER TRACKER" IS A MUST!!!

IT ALLOWS YOU TO KEEP TRACK OF EVERY PURCHASE MADE AND TAKES THE GUESSWORK OUT OF WHAT YOU SHOULD BUY THAT NEXT SILVER ITEM FOR IN ACCORDANCE WITH WHAT'S IN YOUR INVENTORY ALREADY. WHEN THE PRESSURE'S ON AND TIME'S RUNNING OUT ON THAT NEXT BID, THE LAST THING YOU WANT TO DO IS MAKE A MISTAKE AND OVERPAY FOR THAT PURCHASE. THIS TRACKER HAS ENABLED ME TO INPUT THE MAXIMUM AMOUNT I'M WILLING TO PAY FOR AN ITEM WHILE NOT INCREASING MY PURCHASE PRICE.

IF YOU WANT TO BUY AN ITEM UNDER SPOT THIS TRACKER HELPS YOU TO DO THAT. BECOME A SILVER SNIPER TODAY!!!

TWO PAGES FOR INVENTORY AND COMPUTING FUTURE VALUES WHILE ALLOWING YOU TO PLAY AROUND WITH POTENTIAL PURCHASES. JUST PLUG IN YOUR NUMBERS AND ALLOW THE SILVER TRACKER TO COMPUTE THOSE VALUES INSTANTLY. I'VE DONE ALL THE WORK FOR YOU SO YOU CAN MAKE YOUR PURCHASES WITHOUT THE HASSLE.

I'VE INCLUDED A VALUE TRACKER THAT LETS YOU INPUT THE DAILY SPOT PRICE FOR SILVER AND IT COMPUTES THE CURRENT VALUE FOR EACH SIVLER COIN. WHETHER IT'S A WAR NICKEL, MERCURY OR ROOSEVELT DIME, WASHINGTON QUARTER, FRANKLIN, KENNEDY HALVES (BOTH 1964 AND 1965-1970), PEACE AND MORGAN DOLLARS, YOU CAN INSTANTLY SEE WHAT THE VALUE IS AND PURCHASE ACCORDINGLY. YOU SET THE PRICE YOU WANT TO PAY AND LET THE TRACKER DO ALL THE WORK. BECOME A SILVER SNIPER TODAY!!!

IT REALLY IS SILVIVAL!!!

On Mar 9, 2012, at 10:52 PM, Victor wrote:

Simplicity and multi-purpose. It's Silvival, baby! Silvival! Debase the worth of it and I'll use it for survival one way or another!!!

Pioneers used to drop a silver coin in their water to keep it pure on their journeys. I can get a silver ionization system for about $49. Old school becomes relevant again! Silver is a natural anti-microbial. It was used for treating many illnesses prior to the "invention" of penicillin. I'm in love with the stuff!
Victor

Sent via BlackBerry by AT&T

From:
Date: Fri, 9 Mar 2012 22:48:08 -0500
To:
Subject: Re: Sovereign Citizens...

I seem to remember seeing someone polish the bottom of an aluminum soda can with chocolate to make a reflective parabolic mirror to start a fire and it worked. So the silver coin would most likely work. That would be awesome.

I didn't know that about Archimedes. That is just plain manly. I'm going to have to learn how to do that.

B

On Mar 9, 2012, at 10:30 PM, Victor wrote:

Another potential use for silver I've been thinking about is implementing its reflective qualities (it's used in mirrors, you know) for fire-making. Kind of like a magnifying glass, use the coin to reflect the heat from the sun onto the kindling. Archimedes used a large array of mirrors to burn Roman ships during an attack on Syracuse. Actually, Mythbusters recreated this feat on the show and were able to start a fire on a ship 75 feet away. So, something tells me a fire could be started utilizing a pure silver coin. Plus, the conductivity of silver (which just so happens to be used in solar panels) leads me to believe this can be accomplished. I may attempt to find out on the next clear, sunny day. I will report my findings.

When purchasing any coins or looking for silver coins just remember the adage: "1964 and Before!" '64 and before opens the silver door! That's what I say to remember. Happy hunting!

Your vital tool for silver sniping and overall silvival:

Introducing the Silver Tracker:

This first screenshot shows you how to use a simple spreadsheet to compile the basic inventory information you'll need to keep track of your silver purchases.

After the page heading the Silver Tracker is broken down into eight (8) columns. As you can see from the screenshot above those eight categories or columns are:

1) Date (date purchased amount of silver)
2) Ounces (ounces of overall silver purchased with this transaction)
3) Cost (total cost paid for overall silver purchase)

4) Per Oz. (divide column 3 by column 2 to get price paid per ounce of silver)
5) Description (description of the silver purchase made)
6) Rec'd (mark that you received the silver item when you receive it to give you full accountability. Note: once you start purchasing from various places you'll want to ensure you keep track. This is the easiest way I know to do that.)
7) Cost (this column is for totaling the entire amount paid for the amount of silver purchased within a given time frame designated by you)
8) PP/Oz. (this column calculates the average price per ounce of silver during the given time frame designated by you) Note: this is good for keeping track of whether you're paying too much for your purchases and allows you to spot trends. As you can see in the example above, I started to wise up after a few purchases. This tracker is being shared with you as a way to cut your learning curve and hopefully increase your profits. I had to learn the hard way so you don't. You're welcome. ☺

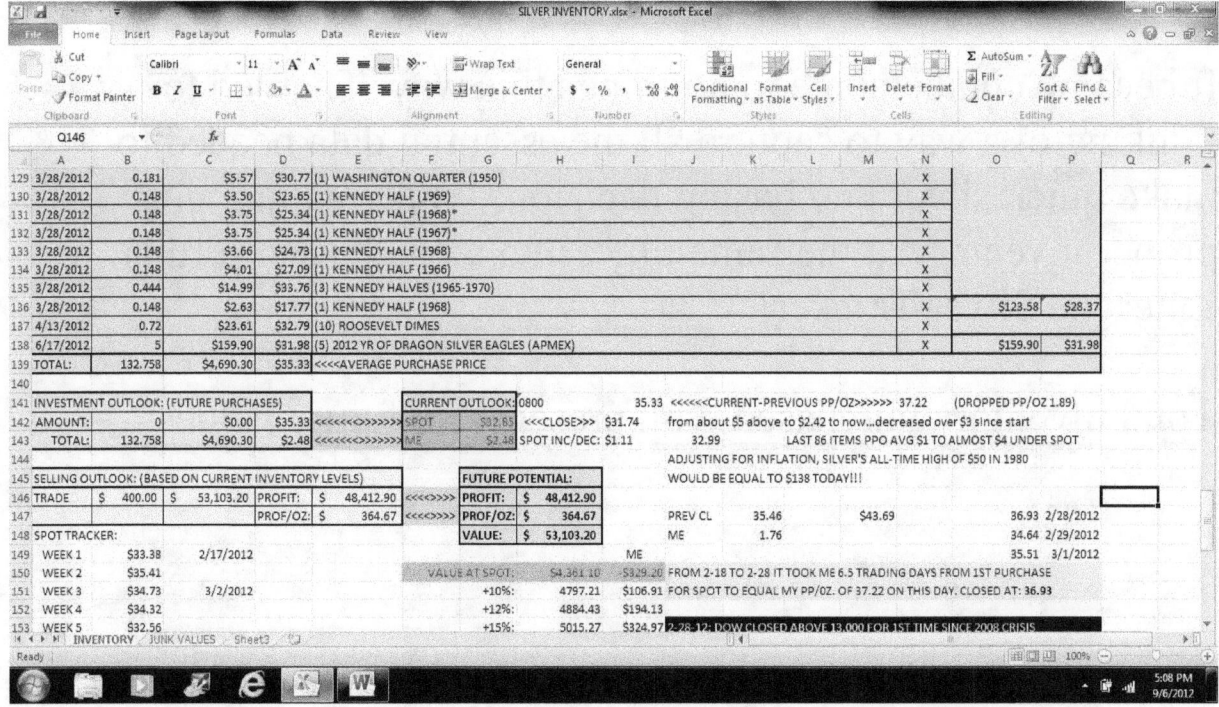

In this screenshot you can see the detailed totals of ounces purchased; total amount paid for those purchases; and the overall price per ounce of silver paid by you. Then below the top table there are various other tables breaking down the calculations in more detail which allow you to track every subsequent silver purchase made. This is essential for maintaining a designated price level for your purchases and allows you to target only those purchases which you deem in accordance with your level of risk.

As you can see from the above screenshot, entering data is simple. It takes all the guesswork out of the purchasing equation for you. As I worked through my silver purchases, it became abundantly clear to minimize the amount of thinking needed to decide whether the purchase would be practical or not. Initially, I had multiple screens open then minimized and was attempting to utilize each one to aid me in purchases.

It became cumbersome to do things this way. That led to thinking of a way to capture all the essential data needed to make quick silver purchasing decisions while maintaining proper inventory at the same time, into a condensed format. Enter the Silver Tracker!

Total inventory purchased with present and future values:

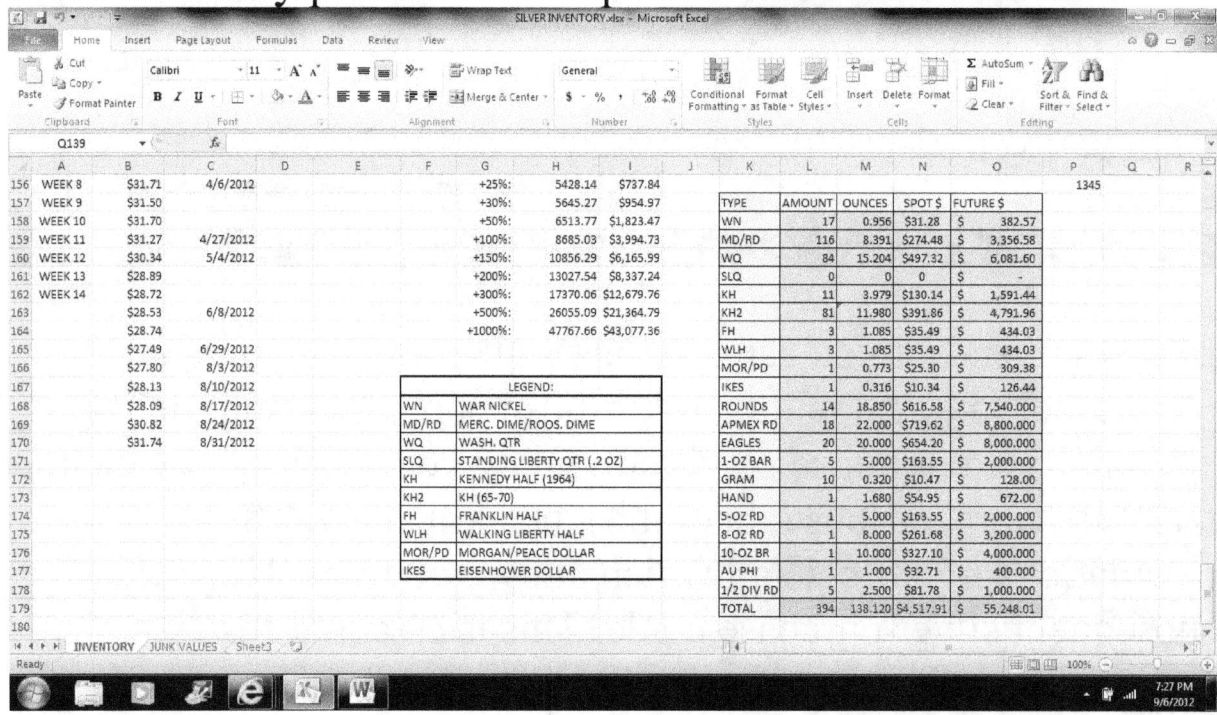

This screenshot shows the bottom portion of the first page. With it one can keep track of all the individual purchases made while keeping track of the current and future values of those purchases. Although individual purchases will need to be added manually upon each purchase, once inputted, everything else is calculated automatically.

Through the Junk Value Table provided in the Silver Tracker on page two, you can always have access to the weights and values for each silver coin. Here is a screenshot of the Junk Value Table:

Junk Value Table:

POTENTIAL OUTLOOK:	CONTENT	WEIGHT	VALUE		QTY	VALUE	
CURRENT SPOT PRICE:	$32.71						
POTENTIAL SPOT:	$40.00			PURCHASE OUTLOOK: BASED ON CURRENT SPOT			
1942-1945 War Nickels	35%	0.05626	$2.25	>>>>>>>	1	$1.84	
1916-1945 Mercury Dimes	90%	0.07234	$2.89	>>>>>>>	1	$2.37	
1946-1964 Roosevelt Dimes	90%	0.07234	$2.89	>>>>>>>	1	$2.37	
1932-1964 Washington Quarters	90%	0.18084	$7.23	>>>>>>>	1	$5.92	STANDING LIBERY QTR=.2 OZ
1916-1947 Walking Liberty Half	90%	0.36169	$14.47	>>>>>>>	1	$11.83	
1948-1963 Franklin Half	90%	0.36169	$14.47	>>>>>>>	1	$11.83	
1964 Kennedy Half	90%	0.36169	$14.47	>>>>>>>	1	$11.83	
1965-1970 Kennedy Half	40%	0.1479	$5.92	>>>>>>>	1	$4.84	
1878-1921 Morgan Dollar	90%	0.77344	$30.94	>>>>>>>	1	$25.30	
1921-1935 Peace Dollar	90%	0.77344	$30.94	>>>>>>>	1	$25.30	
1971-1976-S Eisenhower Dollar	40%	0.3161	$12.64	>>>>>>>	1	$10.34	
				TOTAL:	11	$113.76	
AVG. WEIGHT OF ALL COINS:	0.3162						
(FOR BUYING A JUNK BAG)							

Days upon days of trial and error led to the Silver Tracker being condensed to two spreadsheet pages. The first page contains the overall inventory and every calculation to show overall silver purchased in weight and dollar value. It allows you to see how much you spent and how much your silver is worth. You can play around to see how much your silver would be worth in the future at any set price point you decide to input. With the system set up in the beginning you can see instantaneously, just by entering one figure, the total value of your entire inventory. At any given time and on any given day, values can be tracked.

The second page contains the Junk Value Table. This table is essential for showing current value based on the most recent spot price. Then you can easily see how much each "1964 and before" coin is worth today, tomorrow, and forever. You can do this without having to re-enter the spot price from page one, also. Once it's entered on page one, the value is instantly inputted on page two and all calculations are made.

It becomes quite apparent the Silver Tracker is the ultimate tool for Silvival. Your skills as a Silver Sniper are honed to perfection utilizing this tool.

Chapter 3: On Becoming a Silver Sniper

It was a subtle process as opposed to a definitive goal to become one. But, becoming one proved to be essential for silvival. The act of becoming a silver sniper developed over the course of utilizing the tracker to monitor my purchases.

As my tracking concepts grew my sniping capabilities increased exponentially. The more information I was able to calculate quickly, the better able I was to purchase silver at any quantity at any stated price point I chose. I could instantly see through the use of my Silver Tracker whether that next silver purchase was economical or not. I could set price points. I could play around. All this could be done instantaneously which allowed me to easily decipher which purchases were viable ones and which ones weren't so I could make a bid or quickly move on to the next item.

Once in the bidding process I could play with the numbers to see what my maximum price to pay would be without increasing my overall price per ounce. Unless I wanted to for the sake of making that purchase, I didn't have to pay more than what I calculated beforehand. This proved to be very critical come crunch time as those last few seconds were ticking off the bid timer.

I was in control once I fully developed my tracker. I could easily determine what my price point was and submit my bid accordingly. With confidence! If I got outbid, no problem, I just moved on to the next item. Wash, rinse, repeat!

It really became that simple. Of course, it took a little time to get acclimated to the nuances of the silver purchasing game. But, once you get involved with it and work with it, the system defines itself, and the next thing you know, you're remembering how many ounces of silver each coin contains. Even if you don't get to that point it won't matter because you will always have those values available to you with the Silver Tracker.

Here's how it works:

First you would locate the spot price of silver. I use www.kitco.com for my spot price figure. The spot price is the current value for one ounce of pure silver. You can use any site to get your spot price figure, but I use kitco because I like familiarity. It simplifies the process. I don't have to jump from site to site looking for my info. I've found one that works for my purposes and I stuck with it. Also, they have great information on the entire precious metals market.

Anyway, upon entering their site, you'll want to scroll down looking on the far right side of the site until you come across the silver price. That will be your current spot price for silver and the one you would input in the "CURRENT OUTLOOK" box highlighted in *green* next to "SPOT." Just look for the green box almost direct center on the page right below your inventory table. It's centered on the page to emphasize its importance.

THE SPOT PRICE IS CRITICAL TO ALL VALUES! And, I've simplified entering just this one figure in this one box to calculate ALL values integral to the Silver Tracker. Once the spot price is entered in this box it automatically calculates your current inventory value, the current junk values for silver coins, allows you to compare present and future values, and enables you to utilize the Silver Tracker immediately for the purpose of making equitable purchases. By inputting this one figure into the Silver Tracker, one looking to make the right silver investment is given a competitive advantage.

Simplification to the point of only having to input one figure has made this the only tool a Silver Sniper needs. The Silver Tracker becomes the weapon of choice (actually, the only weapon needed) and the spot price becomes the ammo needed for the Silver Sniper to snipe those deals.

Ok. Now that you have your spot price and have inputted it into the Silver Tracker, the real fun can begin. Up to this point, the Silver Tracker has been revealed as a great way to keep track of your inventory and hinted at as being the "ultimate tool for silvival" and "Silver Sniping." You are now Locked and Loaded! So, let's get to it…

Becoming a Silver Sniper begins with utilizing the Silver Tracker for all purchases. Once the silver spot price is entered, that process can begin immediately. There are various avenues one can take to fill their silver coffers. All of which a Silver

Sniper can masterfully target with ease. I'll use Ebay as the platform of choice for our sniping experience.

Mastering Ebay allows the Silver Sniper to easily target any of the other arenas for silver purchasing. The process on Ebay is simple: search for the silver you want to purchase (rounds, bullion, coins, etc.); target the bidding parameters you feel comfortable with (buy it now, ending soonest, etc.); then get to work setting up your bid.

Be cautious of the items you're looking to purchase. Always do your due diligence. What I mean by this is: define seller parameters you're comfortable with accepting prior to your purchases. This is imperative! Not only does it save you time but it also keeps you from getting burned. For your first few purchases make sure you take your time to follow these guidelines you set for yourself. This will allow you to get familiar with your process and acclimate yourself to the Ebay environment for purchasing silver.

The more you test the waters the easier it becomes and the less you'll set yourself up for a potentially embarrassing purchase. And, believe me, the potential is always there. Especially in the heat of the moment. That's another reason why the Silver Tracker is such an essential tool. By taking all guesswork out of the purchasing equation, the Silver Tracker enables you to go into this arena with a quiet confidence. By knowing what you are willing and able to pay for the purchase up-front, you limit the possibility of buyer's remorse based on paying too much for an item. Or, paying more than you wanted to pay in accordance with your silver-buying goals. The Silver Tracker allows you to remain rational by taking emotion out of the equation.

As the auction timer winds down you will always know how much you can pay and will not fall prey to over-bidding if the Silver Tracker figures are properly inputted and applied. Also, while the bidding is going on, you can be playing with the figures to ensure your maximum purchase amount is adhered to. I usually try to set myself up for a purchase that always brings my average purchase price down. That's what the "INVESTMENT OUTLOOK: (FUTURE PURCHASES)" box is for. You simply input the amount of coins being purchased (their weight) in the first cell and the amount wanting to bid (the price you are willing to pay) in the second cell, then the third cell is automatically computed to give you your new average purchase price.

Starting with Line 145 you can see the "Amount" line:

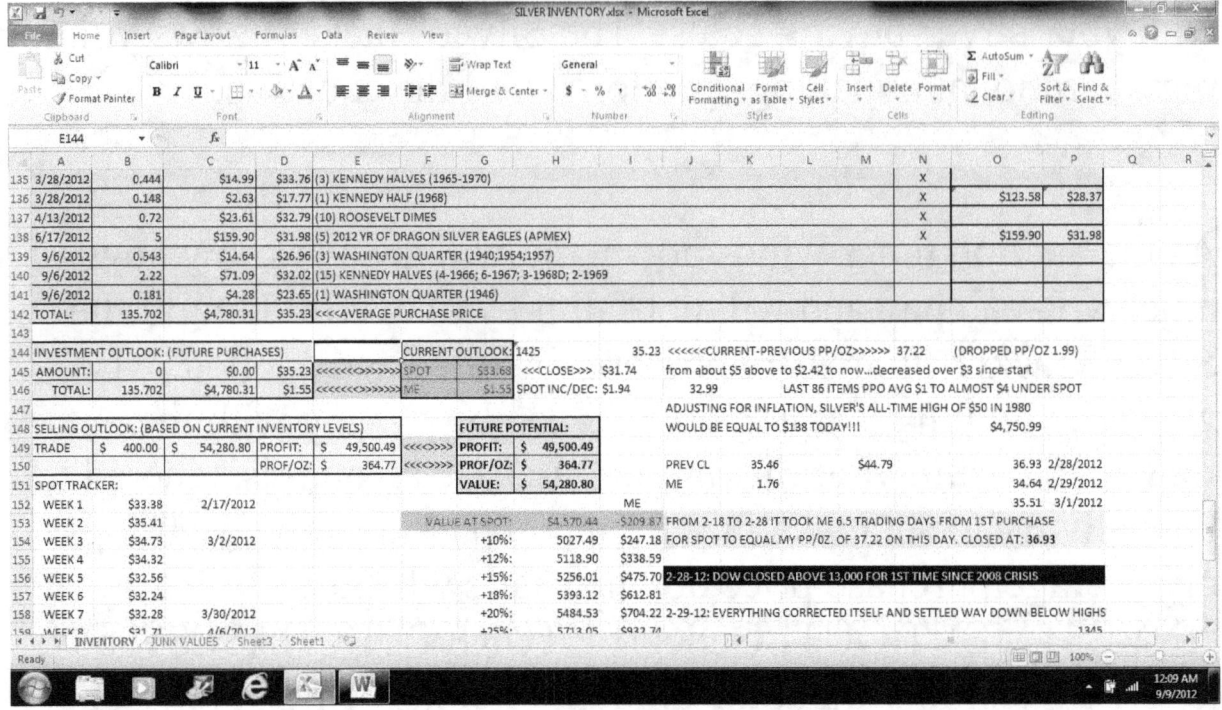

In the above screenshot the Amount line is zeroed out. The Average Purchase Price is shown as $35.23 (the third cell over after "AMOUNT" on line 145). The screenshot below will show an example calculation after values are inputted.

Let's say we're going to purchase (3) Washington Quarters from 1964 and before. By looking at page two (the Junk Value Table) of the Silver Tracker you could input 3 on the Washington Quarter line to give you the current value of 3 of these coins. You would multiply 3 x .181 to get .543 and input this value in the first open Amount line. In the next cell you would enter either the amount of the bid or the amount you are willing to bid.

NOTE: The reason for checking the Junk Value Table first is to immediately see whether the current bid price is higher than the actual value of the coins you're looking to purchase. If the bid price is higher, obviously there's no need to begin entering values into the Investment Outlook table.

Using your discretion, you'll be able to see whether the potential investment is worthy or not once you enter the figures in the Junk Value Table. If you deem it a potentially worthy investment then the next step will be to input the .543 first then the monetary value you're looking to purchase these items at based on current bid asking price and junk value.

Basically, how much are you willing and able to pay? That depends on your personal goals.

Let's look at the example after the values are inputted. For our example, the targeted purchase price for those three quarters is $13.50 (or about $4.50 each). At that purchase price you would lower your Average Purchase Price by $.04, to $35.19. Is that enough for you? That's what you need to decide.

Various figures can be inputted during the bid process:

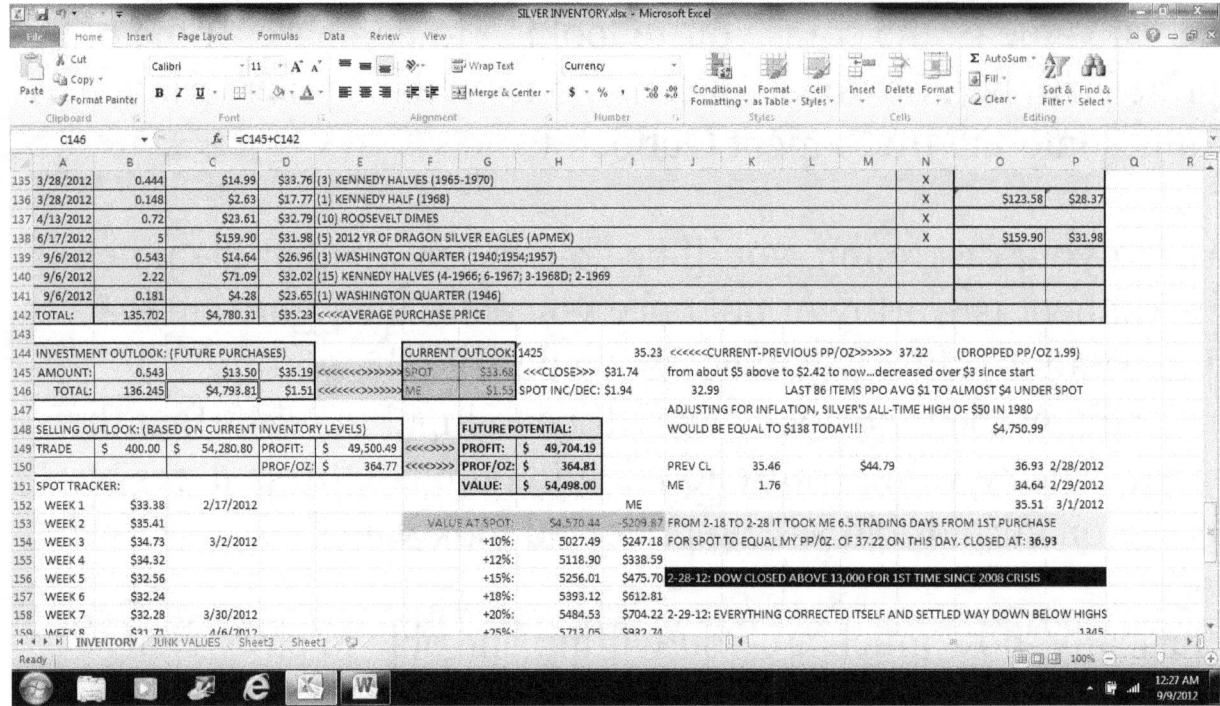

As you can see, various figures can be inputted while the bidding is transpiring, so you can target what your maximum bid should be for the items being bid on during this process. All this is happening in real-time! Once you input the weight values of the silver coins or rounds you're bidding on, then you only have one number to focus on: the purchase price. This is the number you're manipulating during the bidding process. You can change the number in increments allowing you to determine what you're maximum bid will be for each silver purchase. This is what enables you to become the consummate Silver Sniper.

Just like a real sniper trains to hone skills to perfection by narrowing focus and controlling breathing-essentially blocking out all unnecessary distractions, you are implementing those same procedures. You have become the Silver Sniper.

The Silver Sniper utilizes the Silver Tracker to ensure his Silvival. The Silver Tracker allows the Silver Sniper to keep track of his inventory, target his purchases, and maintain a competitive advantage. With the Silver Tracker one can see past, present and future at a glance. Everything is there at your fingertips. Silver Snipers only need to input two figures before entering their battle.

Those two figures are:

1) Current Spot Price of Silver
2) The weight of the silver items being purchased for the present transaction.

After inputting these two values, the Silver Sniper is fully equipped to fight any bidding war. Similar to a sniper in real life, the Silver Sniper is ultimately left with one decision-to engage or not to engage. That decision can be made by entering that one final figure: THE PURCHASE PRICE.

As the sniper factors in the wind, distance, obstacles, among many other variables, so, too does the Silver Sniper. The Silver Tracker takes into account all these other variables. But, upon entering the actual arena for making that current silver purchase, the Silver Tracker serves as the complete arsenal at the Silver

Sniper's disposal. When the bidding war starts and the decision to actually purchase that item is made, though, only one thing matters: THE PURCHASE PRICE.

The Silver Tracker is the essential tool for the Silver Sniper as all the parameters are taken into account then narrowed to one focus (THE PURCHASE PRICE) which enables the Silver Sniper to "take the shot!" One Shot, One Kill! That's the sniper's creed. It's an applicable analogy for the Silver Sniper's mission, too. You really only get that one shot to get it right. By utilizing the Silver Tracker for all your purchases, you'll get it right every time.

The Silver Tracker will make you a Silver Sniper and ultimately ensure your Silvival. Silvival means: utilizing silver as a means to ensure your economic survival and, ultimately, your overall survival.

The hero of this story is the Silver Sniper. That can be you. One focus, Silvival, is the mission. Make it your mission. The Silver Tracker allows the Silver Sniper to accomplish this mission. You can get started immediately.

Purchase the Silver Tracker now! by following this link>>http://www.excelville.com/file/375/SILVER+TRACKER

www.ingramcontent.com/pod-product-compliance
Lightning Source LLC
Chambersburg PA
CBHW080525190526
45169CB00008B/3058